The drawings in this book are by young artists in the United States and Italy. Thank you,

Lauren E. Abernathy
Brian Bailey
Sophie Ban
Davin Bartosch
Amanda Bennett
Noah Charney
Damien Chazelle
Marshall Crumiller
Trenecca D. Doss
Margaret Dyer
Allyson Harper
Greg Hoffman
Tyler Hogan

Jesse Hoover-Dempsey
Olivia Inman
Erin Laughlin
Leeann Lively
Mitch Magdlovitz
Darya Mattes
Elly Motloch
Nicole Mynatt
Leah Neaderthal
Leela Outcalt
Robert Snowden
Daniel Teixeira
Peter Winarsky

from Artrax/Jackson, Community Park Elementary/Princeton, Presbyterian Day School and St. George's Day School/ Memphis, University Park Elementary/Dallas, and University School/Nashville,
with special thanks to Sheila Mattei and her young friends in Florence, Italy.

Cover noodle typography by David Moses

Design and production by Rachel Gabrielleschi and Bob Goode

Photography by

Mike Boatman
Mimi Hurley
Lissa Thompson
Snowden Todd
Jack Tucker

Joe Royer
Peggy Brown
Holly Pedloskey
Natasha Nassar
Lisa Snowden

PASTATIVELY

Italy

By Virginia McLean

To Lisa and Mimi

who made the journey and are the heart of this book.

A Passport to the World Book

Library of Congress Catalog Card Number: 94-065440
ISBN 0-9606046-6-9
First edition, first printing - August 1997
Printed in Hong Kong by South China Printing.

Redbird Press, Inc.,   P. O. Box 11441,   Memphis, TN 38111,   (901)323-2233

My name is Charlie. It doesn't sound very Italian, but I am, part Italian and part American. Every Saturday my mother's radio is tuned to opera live from the Met, and almost every day my family eats some kind of pasta.

Nonna, my great-grandmother, came to New York a long time ago. She lives with us now,

and lots of days, late in the afternoon, I go into her room. I sit up on her bed, and she sits in her favorite chair and tells me her memories — stories about growing up in Italy, about my family and the town where she lived, stories about people I've never met and places I've never been. Or at least that was the case until last summer.

Aunt Patrizia,
that's Pa-treat´-zee-ah,
she's my mom's
sister, and she lives
in Italy, in the
capital city Rome.
She invited me to
come for a visit.

When the plane
landed, a man in a green
uniform checked my
passport and pointed me
toward a huge room, full
of people.

I spotted Aunt
Patrizia almost
immediately. She looks a
lot like my mom. Their
brown hair curls with a
mind of its own, and,
when they smile, their
eyes seem to laugh.

There were hugs and
kisses and pats. Then
we picked up my bag,
put it into the back of
her car, and headed for
the city.

It didn't take long to
realize that this wasn't
going to be just a
trip to visit my
family.

means both hello and good-bye.

"And Italy is so old and so new at the same time." With that Aunt Patrizia parked her car, got out, and led me around a corner.

Aunt Patrizia makes movies, and she knows a whole lot.

"Italy is an amazing place," she said. "You'll see. It has two tiny countries inside it, five different police forces, three active volcanoes, money that's counted in huge numbers with strings of 0000s, a museum about nothing but pasta, and one word that

"These stones are the remains of a much older Rome," she said, "one of history's few superpowers. Way back, around the year 1AD, the Romans who lived here spoke a language called Latin and ruled an empire that spread around the whole Mediterranean Sea.

"This is the Forum. It was their main public meeting place and the center of

their government. Soldiers returning from battle marched through its great stone arches and past its pillared temples. Chariots drove its roads, and people crowded into its shops.

There were no signs reading DO NOT TOUCH, so I rubbed my hand on a broken column. I figured

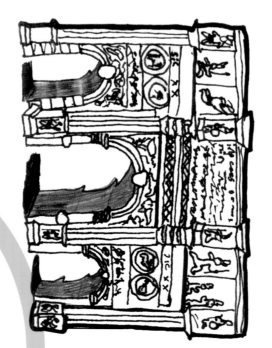

out faded dates carved in Roman numerals and walked where Roman boys had passed in their togas.

I watched two girls sipping water from a fountain where Roman soldiers may have drunk. I took a sip. It was fresh and cool.

I climbed in the Colosseum, their sports stadium. It used to seat 90,000 people. Now its seats are gone and grass grows between its stones. It's empty except for visitors like me and some curious stray cats. But, as I stood here, I could imagine crowds cheering as men called gladiators fought for their lives.

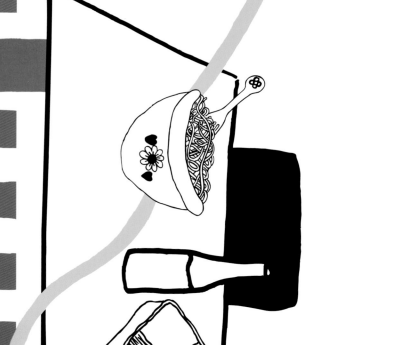

When we got to Aunt Patrizia's apartment, it was two o'clock, time for lunch. In Italy it's called *pranzo* (prahn´-zoh), and it's the biggest meal of the day.

Lots of the family were there to meet me — Uncle Mario and his family, they live down the street;

and Cousin Elena and her family, they live upstairs above Aunt Patrizia. Everyone hugged and kissed everyone else. I didn't feel like a stranger at all.

My family spoke English so I could understand, but every now and then they'd slip into Italian. I listened to the sounds and watched their hands and faces, always moving. I wanted to be able to speak Italian, too.

We sat together around a big table and ate lots of food — salami, spaghetti, roast chicken, baked fish, eggplant, tomatoes, string beans, cheese, and fresh pears and peaches — served in courses with bottles of mineral water and wine on the table.

Most days everyone takes a nap after lunch, even the adults, but not today. We ate and talked and laughed for hours.

The next day Cousin Francesco invited me to a camp at his church. That's where Italian kids go in the summer and after school in the winter. We played soccer and basketball and painted posters for a carnival. I had a great time.

Most of Francesco's friends watch American TV shows and listen to rock music, so they already know lots about the United States. They wear tennis shoes, play video games, and love sports. I could've been at home, almost. In Italy they go to school six days a week; that means on Saturdays, too.

Francesco is fourteen, and he can drive a motorcycle. Late in the afternoons we'd ride to meet his friends at an outdoor cafe, and some nights, about ten o'clock, we'd go out for pizza. Nobody goes to sleep early in Italy.

At least once each day either Aunt Patrizia or Francesco would show me something new. Usually, it was old; I mean really old, a lot older than at home. After a while I wanted to put these things and the people who'd lived here into some kind of order. "That's what history is about," Aunt Patrizia said, "and time is just a way to measure change."

900-396 BC - Etruscans, wealthy iron traders, rule most of Italy and write in a language that still hasn't been decoded.

509 BC - Romans overthrow Etruscans, and during the next 200 years, will conquer most of Italy; later, the world.

218 BC - Hannibal, a daring general from the powerful north African state of Carthage, leads troops into Italy on elephant-back to fight the Romans for control of the Mediterranean. Hannibal wins this time, but eventually Rome will win the Punic Wars.

27 BC - Augustus Caesar becomes the first Roman Emperor.

6 - 4 BC - Between these years, Christ is born in Bethlehem, now part of the Roman Empire. Christianity will spread throughout the Empire.

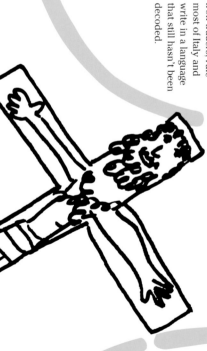

410 AD - Tribes invade from the north, and the Roman Empire falls apart. Wars follow. People flee to the countryside and live in castles for protection. During the next 1500 years, different groups and countries will fight to control pieces of Italy.

1095 AD - Crusaders leave Italy to recapture the Holy Land.

c.1325-1527 AD - Italy's towns grow and become world centers of learning, trade, and art. These years, named the Renaissance, are a time of curiosity and learning, knowledge about the past, new ideas, new technology, new styles, and new art.

1492 AD - Columbus, an Italian, sails to America.

1776 AD - The United States of America, named after Italian Amerigo Vespucci, declares itself a country.

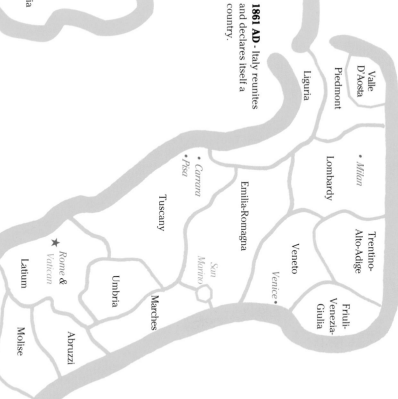

Sardinia

Sicily

Valle D'Aosta
Piedmont

Liguria

· Milan
Lombardy

Trentino-Alto-Adige

Emilia-Romagna

Veneto

Friuli-Venezia-Giulia

Venice ·

· Carrara
· Pisa

Tuscany

San Marino

★
Rome & Vatican

Latium

Umbria

Marches

· Campania
· Pompeii

Abruzzi

Molise

Calabria

Basilicata

Apulia

1861 AD - Italy reunites and declares itself a country.

"Each city and region here is like a piece in a puzzle," Aunt Patrizia said, "a puzzle torn apart almost 1600 years ago and just recently reassembled. Each area still has its own flag, way of speaking, favorite foods, music, folk tales, even games."

Aunt Patrizia wanted me to see the different pieces during the summer. "There's an old saying that all roads lead to Rome. We'll take those in reverse," she joked.

Lots of weekends we'd head out in her car, but, for longer trips, we usually took the train. I loved the trains. We'd get reserved seats in a compartment and take along a picnic. Everyone was friendly. I think they like kids a lot in Italy.

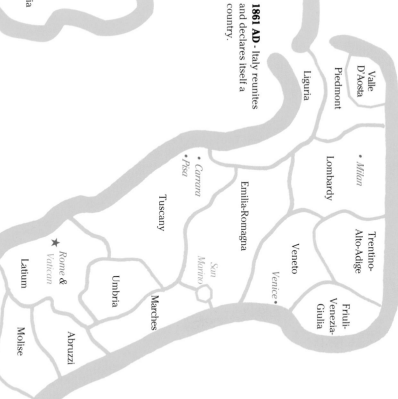

I saw the world's first shopping mall in Milan and mountains near Carrara where marble quarries glisten like snow.

During the summer we went to Sicily, the ball Italy's boot is kicking, the biggest island in the Mediterranean Sea; and to Pompeii, a whole town whose buildings and people were buried by a volcano.

We went to Venice, a city built on top of the ocean where the streets are water and the speed limit is three miles per hour; and to Pisa where some say Galileo tested gravity from a bell tower that still stands, but just barely.

When we went south, life seemed slower, more old-fashioned. Farmers grow olives, tomatoes, oranges, and wheat. Shepherds tend sheep on quiet hillsides.

Greek temples, used now only by wedding photographers, stand in lonely fields, long ago abandoned by the Greeks who came here to set up trading colonies.

Up north life moves faster. Business is booming. Fancy cheeses and chocolates and some of the world's sleekest cars and clothes are made here now in cities long famous as centers of art, trade, and learning.

As we traveled I saw that Aunt Patrizia was right. Each piece of Italy is different, but all over the country I kept seeing towns built on top of mountains, surrounded by wheat fields, vineyards, olive groves, or sometimes even by fields of sunflowers.

In each town, I saw squares with their fountains and statues and always people walking and chatting and shopping, stopping for a cup of thick dark Italian coffee or an ice cream cone.

There are several different types of ice cream, like *granita* (grah-nee-´tah) which is icy and *gelato* (jah-lah-´toe) which is creamy, and more flavors to choose from

I think it's the best ice cream in the whole world.

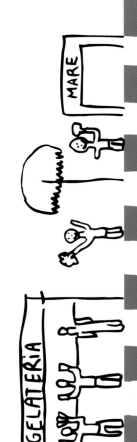

than I ever dreamed of, all the ones I'm used to, plus flavors like persimmon, fig, and prickly pear. You can pick one flavor or have it *metà e metà* (meh´-tah ay meh´-tah). That means half one kind and half another.

"All of Italy is a delight to the senses —
eyes, ears, mouth, and hands." That's what
Aunt Patrizia says. "Great food, music,
art, and architecture."

I agree.

At night we'd hear accordion and
violin music outside in the streets and
symphonies and operas in majestic
old theaters.

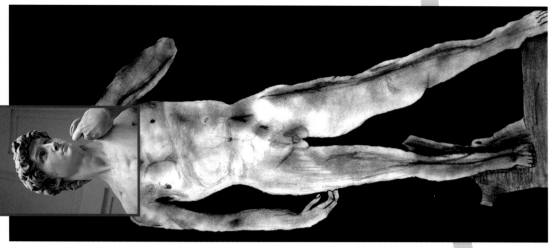

No matter what size the town or city, it always had a famous building, painting, or sculpture for us to see, works by artists like Michelangelo, Raphael, Donatello, and Leonardo da Vinci. What beautiful things Italian hands have made!

Wherever we traveled we were always near both the mountains and the sea. In Italy you don't get far from either.

We ate lunch on terraces built out over the ocean and swam in turquoise water where fishermen still go about their business the way it's been done for thousands of years.

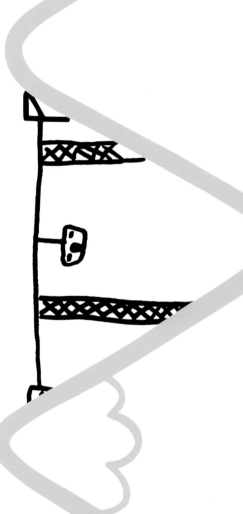

We had picnics and collected wild mushrooms in the mountains where skiers come in the winter and bikers in the summer.

And everywhere we went there were churches, big ones and little ones, with beautiful altars and bells and angels, always angels.

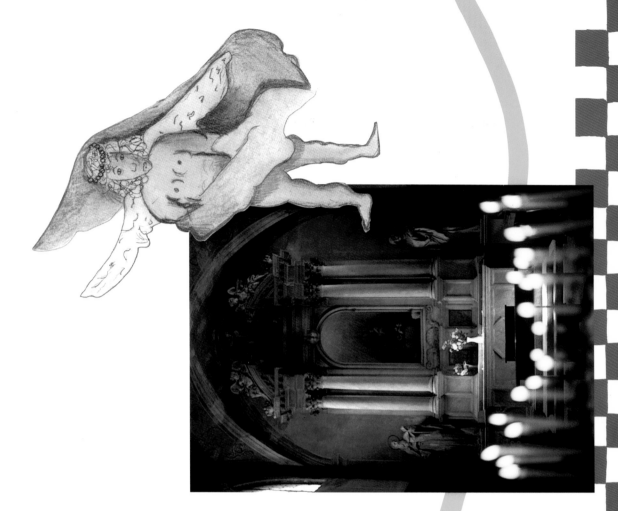

For a long time there was only one kind of Christian church in Europe, the Catholic Church. The Pope is its head. Today he lives in the Vatican, a tiny country about the size of a golf course, inside the city of Rome. The Vatican has its own flag, prints its own money and stamps, and has its own 100-man army.

They're from Switzerland and carry ancient weapons. Aunt Patrizia thinks they may carry hidden machine guns, too.

St. Peter's Cathedral is here. It's HUGE. I climbed way up inside the dome, 537 steps; I counted.

The Pope came out on a balcony to bless us as we gathered with thousands of Christians in the enormous square in front of the cathedral. With a twinge in my heart I squeezed the two rosaries I'd bought, one for Mom and one for Nonna.

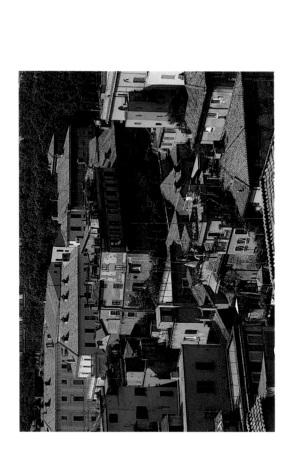

Some afternoons I'd sit on Aunt Patrizia's roof garden
and try to count the crosses and domes. I don't believe
anybody, even the Pope, knows how many
churches are in Rome, much less in Italy.

And festivals, there are so many. Everywhere we went, something was being or had been or was about to be celebrated.

The whole month of May is dedicated to Mary, the mother of Christ. She's the official saint of Italy, but towns and cities also have their own special saints and festivals in their honor.

There are parades and horse races, fireworks and feasts, balls and the blessing of boats — festivals that started hundreds of years ago and still go on in the same way today.

All the traditions seemed to jumble time and to toss the generations of my family like a bowl of noodles.

Uncle Alessandro is a sculptor like his father and grandfather before him. My cousin sleeps in the bed he was born in and goes to the church where his

parents were married. Each Saturday, Cousin Elena puts flowers on the graves of her great-great-grandparents.

In Italy you can't ignore time or history or death. You see and feel the changes. Aunt Patrizia says that's why Italians enjoy life so much.

Maybe she's right. About

six o'clock in the evening whole towns move outside. It's

an old custom, the *passeggiata* (pahs-sed-jah´-tah). Around

squares nuns stop to chat with

friends; men sit having a cool

drink, playing cards,

talking politics, and watching girls go by; kids hang out, ride

bikes, and play ball; women stroll, chatting and gossiping.

Each group closes out the world from its conversation, and

yet each knows that everyone is watching everyone else.

The *passeggiata* is different in big cities and little towns, in northern and southern Italy. In some places, it's almost disappeared. But all over Italy there seems to be a feeling that it's good to be alive. Italians find a hand to hold, a reason to celebrate, a costume to wear, and there is almost always a dish of pasta on the table.

Here's a recipe for one of my favorite pasta dishes. It has a funny name that means mean and angry. It's hot and spicy.

Buon appetito!

Penne all'Arrabbiata (for 4)

1 lb. dried *penne*
1/4 C extra virgin olive oil
2 oz. sliced *pancetta* (pan-chet 'tah), cut into strips (optional)
1/2 t. garlic, chopped finely
3 C fresh or canned tomatoes, peeled, seeded, & chopped
1/2 t. red pepper flakes
salt
12 leaves fresh basil , torn
4 T Parmesan cheese, freshly grated

Put oil and *pancetta* in a large skillet over medium heat. Cook until it is browned but not crisp. Add garlic and stir until it sizzles. Add tomatoes, red pepper, and 1/4 t. salt. Reduce heat and simmer 30 minutes. Stir in basil and remove skillet from heat.

While sauce is simmering, put 4 qts of water in a large pot and bring to a boil. Stir in 1/2 T salt and the *penne*. Cook *al dente*, according to directions on the package. That means it stays chewy.

Drain the *penne* and add it to the sauce. Stir in the grated cheese. Taste and serve.

There are so many different kinds of pasta.
Some say at least six hundred, with new types
being made every day, all shapes and sizes
and colors with different sauces and names
that paint their own pictures.

Some say pasta was first made in China;
others claim in Persia. But today, there's no
doubt about it — pasta is as Italian as
hamburgers are American.

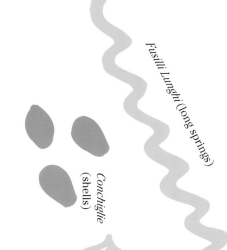

Fusilli Lunghi (long springs)

Conchiglie (shells)

Ruote (wheels)

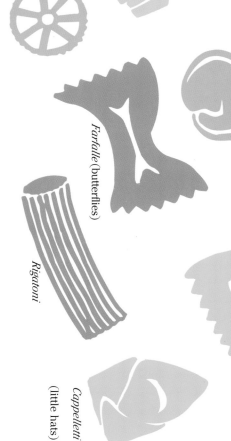

Tortellini

Farfalle (butterflies)

Rigatoni

Anelli (rings)

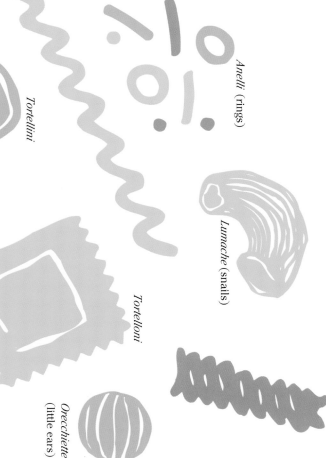

Lumache (snails)

Tortelloni

Fusilli (springs)

Orecchiette (little ears)

Cappelletti (little hats)

By the end of the summer I understood exactly what she meant. And now, late in the afternoons, when Nonna and I look at old photographs and talk about Italy, I know that Italy is more than a place. It's a way of life, a joy in living. I see it in Nonna,

And there's no doubt about me and my family, either. Each of us is different and special, as different as the types of pasta. Today some of us live in America; some, in Italy. But each of us is still Italian, as Aunt Patrizia likes to say, "pastatively Italian."

Capelli D'Angelo (angel hair)

Raviolini

Penne (pens)

Radiatori (radiators)

Fettuccine

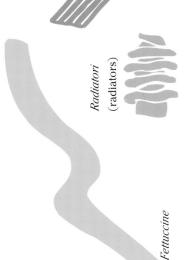

Cavatappi (corkscrews)

and I see it in me, too.